RE 627H RAINBOWFI

CW01667820

ONTENTS

Distributed in the UNITED STATES by T.F.H. Publications, Inc., 1 TFH Plaza, Neptune City, NJ 07753; on the Internet at www.tfh.com; in CANADA by Rolf C. Hagen Inc., 3225 Sartelon St., Montreal, Quebec H4R 1E8; Pet Trade by H & L Pet Supplies Inc., 27 Kingston Crescent, Kitchener, Ontario N2B 2T6; in ENGLAND by T.F.H. Publications, PO Box 74, Havant PO9 5TT; in AUSTRALIA AND THE SOUTH PACIFIC by T.F.H. (Australia), Pty. Ltd., Box 149, Brookvale 2100 N.S.W., Australia; in NEW ZEALAND by Brooklands Aquarium Ltd., 5 McGiven Drive, New Plymouth, RD1 New Zealand; in SOUTH AFRICA by Rolf C. Hagen S.A. (PTY.) LTD., P.O. Box 201199, Durban North 4016, South Africa; in JAPAN by T.F.H. Publications. Published by T.F.H. Publications, Inc.

MANUFACTURED IN THE
UNITED STATES OF AMERICA
BY T.F.H. PUBLICATIONS, INC.

INTRODUCTION

I started keeping tropical fish in 1969 when I was given my first tropical aquarium as a birthday present. Almost from the start I had a few rainbowfishes in it, and they have continued to play an important part in my fishkeeping ever since. In fact one of the very first egglayers I bred was a rainbowfish. At the time it was being called *Melanotaenia nigrans*, but it was in fact probably *Melanotaenia duboulayi* or a subspecies of *Melanotaenia splendida*. This first spawning took place in the fall of 1974, and the following year I started winning prizes at fish shows with a breeder's team of these fish.

Melanotaenia duboulayi, shown above, was called *Melanotaenia nigrans* when rainbowfishes were first kept.

PHOTO BY DR. HERBERT R. AXELROD.

With this success I became all fired up to work with some of the other rainbows. My books listed at least three other species as being available in the European hobby at that time. Of these I had seen only one, but then I had hardly been looking for any others. The fish I could find was *Telmatherina ladigesi*, the Celebes Rainbowfish. It was first introduced to the hobby in 1933 and has been a regular import ever since. This species was soon added to my collection, and the search moved on.

The other two species were more problematic. A photograph of *Melanotaenia maccullochi* was regularly included in the literature, and the species was supposed to have been imported into Europe in 1934, yet despite searching aquatic stores all over the country for the better part of a decade I did not see any in real life until a friend imported some from the continent a few years ago.

The final species available at that time was the Madagascan Rainbowfish, *Bedotia geayi*. This one was around in the hobby but was like gold dust and generally cost a fortune if it was ever available. It took me some time, but I eventually had a chance to work with this species in the late 1970's.

A pair of Madagascan Rainbowfish, *Bedotia geayi*.

PHOTO BY HANS JOACHIM RICHTER.

By that time other species were beginning to make themselves known on the hobby scene. One of the most spectacular was the Red New Guinea Rainbowfish, *Glossolepis incisus*. This one first arrived in England towards the end of the 1970s and proved to be one of the larger species; it can reach sizes in excess of 5 inches. Males have very deep humpbacked bodies and are a lovely rich red color.

The early 1980s saw the introduction of Boeseman's Rainbowfish, *Melanotaenia boesemani*. This one had a bluish-black front part of the body and a rich orangy yellow rear. From then on we started to see new species appearing in the trade just about every year if not every month.

One of my personal favorites appeared at about this time. This was the Forked-tail Rainbowfish, *Pseudomugil furcatus*. Unlike the previously seen rainbows, this was a much smaller species (max. 2 inches) with a long slender body and large bright yellow orange winglike fins. *P. furcatus* proved to be a little more difficult to breed than the previous species but soon became a favorite with those aquarists who work with killifishes. This is because *P. furcatus* and many of the killies breed in a similar fashion, with just an egg or two laid every day.

A group of *Glossolepis incisus*. They grow to about 5 inches in length. The males are more colorful than females.

PHOTO BY HEINRICH STOLZ.

A female *Melanotaenia boesemani.*

PHOTO BY HANS JOACHIM RICHTER.

The eggs are large and can be handled in just the same way as killifish eggs are.

Today my fish house contains several different species of rainbowfishes including the Dwarf Neon Rainbowfish, *Melanotaenia praecox.* This stunning animal was first imported into Europe in 1992, and it soon became the most desirable rainbow of all time. Once you see a school of this species you will realize why. Both sexes have a lovely blue body with red-to-orange fins. They only grow to about 2.5 inches long and thus are one of the smaller species in their genus. They are peaceful and relatively hardy, and they fit in well in a community aquarium of small to medium-size fish. In other words, like all other rainbowfishes, they are perfect aquarium fish.

Looking to the future, it appears that the explosion of available rainbowfish species will continue well into the next millennium. Dr. Gerald R. Allen, who has been behind many of the new imports and discoveries, has been trying to obtain sufficient finances and permits to study the fishes of Irian Jaya. This is the western half of New Guinea; it is governed by Indonesia and in the past has been a rich source of new species. It now looks as if this project is up and running, so we should see many new species coming from this area.

Another part of Indonesia is also rich in rainbowfishes and has been almost untouched by fish collectors. This is the Island of Sulawesi. We have experience in the hobby of only one species of rainbow from this island, yet there are a further 15 species in the family known to occur on the island. Some of them are supposed to be bright blue, whereas others are iridescent gold or even black.

Looking further afield, the Madagascan Rainbowfish belongs to a family that contains about 165 species. Many of them are marine fishes, but some occur in fresh water and would make excellent aquarium fish if they were ever introduced to the hobby. In the past I have worked with one of them, a species of *Chirostoma* that occurs in Mexico. It was a lovely golden color and proved to be quite hardy once it

Habitat of *Chilatherina* near Bewoni, Papua New Guinea.

PHOTO BY DR. GERALD R. ALLEN.

An ideal habitat of rainbowfishes is Lake Holmes in the lower Mamberamo River system in Irian Jaya.

PHOTO BY DR. GERALD R. ALLEN.

was established in my tanks. The problem I had was that only males survived the journey back to my home in England, which makes breeding them a little difficult. This was a real pity, because some of these species are supposed to internally fertilize their eggs like the popular aquarium livebearers.

From this I think you can see the world of rainbowfishes takes in far more territory than just Australia. In the past that country has been the main source of rainbowfishes in the hobby, but over the last decade or so we have seen some of the lovely New Guinea species making their appearance—and there are many more to follow. This is an exciting time to be in the rainbowfish hobby, and I hope you gain as much pleasure from working with these lovely animals as I have.

CLASSIFICATION AND DISTRIBUTION IN THE WORLD

Defining exactly what is a "rainbowfish" is a little difficult. Many aquarists have tended to call any fish with two dorsal fins a "rainbowfish," yet many non-rainbowfish species have this characteristic. Recently some scientists have attributed this common name to a single family (Melanotaeniidae) while acknowledging the Sulawesi rainbowfishes as belonging to another group that has a claim to the same common name. This ignores a fish like the Madagascan Rainbowfish, which belongs to the family Atherinidae. Atherinids are generally called silversides, so in theory the common name for *Bedotia geayi* should be Madagascan Silverside. Yet nobody in the aquarium hobby would know what you are talking about! This is just one reason why scientific names are used so much in literature—it is the only way we all know what we are talking about.

The scientific classification of the rainbowfishes (in common with many other groups of fish) has undergone major upheavals

Chilatherina axelrodi.

PHOTO BY DR. GERALD R. ALLEN.

A male *Melanotaenia boesemani* not in breeding dress.

PHOTO BY HANS JOACHIM RICHTER.

over the years. It is well beyond the scope of this book to go into any great depth on this subject, but this is how things stand at the moment:

ORDER ATHERINIFORMES

Family - Atherinidae

Contains approximately 165 species that are distributed throughout the world. Most are found in marine or brackish water, but some are found in freshwater habitats in areas not normally associated with rainbows, e.g.. 18 species of *Chirostoma* from Mexico.

Family - Dentatherinidae

This family contains only one species, which comes from the western Pacific Ocean.

Family - Melanotaeniidae

Melanotaeniidae contains the bulk of the rainbowfishes currently being kept . At present there are 53 species in the family, but more are expected to be discovered in the coming years. They are found only in Australia and New Guinea, where they inhabit fresh water.

Family - Notocheiridae

The six species contained in this family come from tropical and temperate seas around the world.

Family - Phallostethidae

This family is made up of about 20 species that are found in fresh and brackish waters of Southeast Asia. They are a very strange group; they lack pelvic fins, and in the males this part of the

A magnificent male *Pseudomugil conniae* prancing with outstretched fins.
PHOTO BY GUNTER SCHMIDA.

skeleton has developed into a copulatory organ called a priapium. In the female the urogenital opening is also below the throat.

Family - Pseudomugilidae

A family of 15 species from Australia and New Guinea which occur in brackish and fresh waters. All are rather small and can be difficult to maintain in captivity.

Family - Telmatherinidae

Seventeen known species make up this family. At present all but one species are thought to occur on the island of Sulawesi, where they inhabit freshwater rivers, lakes, and streams. One of these is thought to live in brackish-water habitats. Apart from the well known Celebes Rainbowfish, *Telmatherina ladigesi,* several other species in this group have a great deal of potential as aquarium fishes. Most notable of these is *Tominanga sanguicauda.* Males of this species are either solid blue or red with a red caudal and blue or red dorsal, anal, and pelvic fins. A truly beautiful fish that would be an instant hit if it were ever introduced to the aquarium hobby.

Schnepper Creek near Tin Can Bay, Queensland, Australia is typical of the habitat of many rainbowfishes.

PHOTO BY DR. GERALD R. ALLEN.

Telmatherina ladigesi, two males and one female.

PHOTO BY MP&C PIEDNOIR.

Rainbow habitat in stream form near Ajamaru Valley, New Guinea. This stream yielded *Melanotaenia boesemani* and a new blue-eye still to be described.

PHOTO BY DR. GERALD R. ALLEN.

AQUARIUM CONDITIONS

RAINBOWS IN THE WILD

With such a widespread and diverse group of fishes it is unlikely there will be a typical type of habitat in which all species are found. Reading through the literature available on this subject and comparing it with my own experiences, it soon becomes clear, however, that there is a "typical" habitat that rainbows inhabit. There are of course some exceptional species living in other types of habitat, but the following description fits the majority of the habitats these fishes come from.

First of all the water is generally clean, clear, and highly oxygenated, with little in the way of turbidity. Most live in flowing rivers and streams, but some also come from large lakes and small ponds. Vegetation along the banks, both growing in and hanging down into the water, is common, and in many cases the water is hard and slightly alkaline rather than soft and acidic.

Collecting under these conditions is generally best done with a seine net rather than a hand or dip net. This is because the fish can easily see you coming

Seining for Red Rainbows in Lake Sentani, Pápua New Guinea.

PHOTO BY DR. GERALD R. ALLEN.

PHOTO BY DR. GERALD R. ALLEN.

with either of these small nets but tend to become confused and entrapped by the larger seine net. Care should be taken when collecting this way, however, because it is easy to damage fish in a seine net. Also, if a large number of fish are caught in one sweep with the net some of them will be seriously harmed while out of the water being sorted. In this case, sort for a maximum of three minutes before releasing all the surplus fish—and next time make a shorter sweep and catch fewer fish. Obviously, if you are a scientist this is not a problem, because most of the collected fish will be preserved rather than kept alive, but if you are an aquarist looking for a few fish to start a breeding colony then careful handling out in the field is essential if you are to be successful.

RAINBOWS IN THE COMMUNITY AQUARIUM.

Rainbows are among the most obliging fishes in that they will fit in well with most other species. Apart from courting males, which can become a little rough at times, they do not seem to have an aggressive bone in their bodies. Even so, they are lively fishes and can become too much for very slow-moving or timid species.

My very first aquarium was much like everybody else's and contained a mixed group of hardy fishes. In the beginning it housed a pair of Guppies, a pair of Platies, a small group of Neon Tetras, and a couple of *Corydoras* catfish. Later I added more fish as the aquarium filtration system matured, and in this second wave I included my first pair of rainbows. They settled in perfectly well with the other fishes in the aquarium and lived for many years in this setup.

When selecting rainbows to be housed in a community aquarium it is important to think of how the different fishes will interact with each other. If you have a tank containing mostly small to medium-size species like Neon Tetras, Platies and Guppies, then it is wise to pick rainbows that are fully grown when only a couple of inches long. Suitable species for this sort of tank would be *Melanotaenia maccullochi*, *Melanotaenia praecox*, and *Pseudomugil furcatus*. If only very small fishes are housed in your community tank, you should look for the tiny species like *Pseudomugil gertrudae*, *Iriatherina werneri*, and *Pseudomugil mellis*. These species can be hard to find, but I have seen all of them offered through normal trade outlets in both Europe and America in the last few years.

Communities of peaceful medium-size to larger fishes make fine homes for most of the other rainbows, which generally grow to between 4 and 6 inches. While they can be housed with smaller fishes without too many problems, if there is a large size

Lake Sentani, Papua New Guinea. Most lakes and streams provide suitable habitats for rainbows of one kind or another.

difference the rainbows may try to eat their small tankmates or at the very least push them out of the way at feeding time. It is therefore better to house them in tanks with fishes about the same size as they are.

In the wild rainbows tend to live in large schools rather than as single individuals. For this reason it is important to keep them in a group of about 6 to 10 individuals if they are to be really happy. Ideally all fish in the group should be of the same species, but in most cases a mixed bag of rainbows will get along just fine.

Melanotaenia maccullochi.

PHOTO BY HANS JOACHIM RICHTER.

WATER QUALITY

One of the most important factors in keeping rainbows healthy and happy is the water quality. They can tolerate a wide range of pH and hardness, but if the oxygen content drops or dissolved waste products like ammonia have a chance to build up the rainbows will be the first fishes in trouble. For this reason it is important not to overcrowd them.

When trying to assess how many rainbows you can house in a particular aquarium there is a simple formula to follow. First of all, work out the surface area of the tank. To do this just multiply the length by the width in inches. For a 24" x 12" tank this would work out to be 288 square inches of surface area. Divide this by 8, which will give you the number of inches of fish the tank can hold, in this case 36. Now this is not a figure of how many fish you can have, nor is it even a figure of how many inches of body length of fish you can have. It is, in fact, a figure of how many inches of body length of fish the tank can hold *bearing in mind the maximum adult size each fish will reach.*

Iriatherina werneri.

PHOTO BY HANS JOACHIM RICHTER.

So if you buy a group of 6 *Glossolepis incisus* which are only 2 inches long when you buy them, you have to take account of the fact they will grow to 5 inches long when fully adult. That means they will take up 30 inches of your 36-inch allowance, which will leave only enough room to add a couple of *Corydoras* catfish to keep the bottom clean.

Another important fact to remember with rainbows is that they are basically surface to mid-water swimmers. This means they will only rarely follow food to the bottom of the tank, and then only half-heartedly. So when choosing companions for rainbows, make sure you include a few bottom dwellers to clean up any leftover food that reaches the bottom. *Corydoras* catfish are ideal for this job, but so are coolie loaches and some of the *Botia* species. Peaceful dwarf cichlids can also be used.

The choice of filtration for any community tank can be a little daunting nowadays. There are so many alternatives on the market, some of which sound as if you

need a degree in chemistry to understand how they work. Personally I have never placed too much emphasis on this sort of gadgetry. The reason for this is that I live in a small village out in the middle of nowhere. Power outages are something we expect several times during every winter, so if my fish depended on complicated filtration and aeration systems I would be in grave danger of losing them.

If you keep the stocking levels down to those already quoted, then all you need is a small internal power filter or an undergravel filter. My preference is to include an internal power filter in any tank that permanently houses adult rainbows. This is because power filters produce plenty of water movement and are efficient mechanical filters as well. Rainbows love this water movement and will swim against it much of the day. These filters also have some biological action and are easy to keep clean, which in a setup the size of mine is a real boon.

Entitled *WATER COLOR PANORAMA* by the brilliant Takashi Amano, this is an ideal tank set up for most rainbowfishes. This photo is from Amano's book NATURE AQUARIUM WORLD, Book 3.

PHOTO BY TAKASHI AMANO.

One of the most important chores any aquarist must perform if his fish are to remain healthy is regular partial water changes. Most authors suggest about a fifth of the water should be changed every week or two. With good filtration this will be adequate for most species of fish. Rainbows, however, in my experience do better the more fresh water they come in contact with. I aim to change four-fifths of the water in my tanks every week. This is replaced with tapwater of the same temperature, hardness, and pH. In my area we have some chlorine added to the tapwater, but no chloramine. This means I can get away without using an aquarium water conditioner. In other areas you may find that either the level of chlorine is too high or that chloramine has been added, in which case you will have to add a conditioner to your tapwater to make it safe for use with fishes. Check with your local aquarium shop to be sure.

PLANTS IN THE RAINBOWFISH AQUARIUM

Over the years my fishkeeping has gone through various phases in which aquatic plants have been either a major feature of the setup or just about absent from it. Without doubt they are not essential to keeping fishes healthy, but in recent years I have come to believe they are certainly appreciated by many species. Nowadays most of the otherwise bare tanks in my fish room have a pot or two of plants growing in them. In breeding tanks Java

Java Moss, *Vesicularia dubyana*, is suitable for the rainbowfish tank.

PHOTO BY MP&C PIEDNOIR.

The Four-leafed Clover, *Marsilea quadrifolia.*

PHOTO BY RUDA ZUKAL.

Moss is often used as a spawning medium, and if pairs of rainbows are spawning in a planted community tank they will always select a few of the fine-leafed plants in which to lay their eggs. In addition the beautiful green backdrop that plants make in an aquarium also helps show off your fishes' colors to their best effect. Also, provided that growing plants are used and not plastic ones, they help keep the buildup of nitrates under control.

THE RAINBOWFISH TANK.

So far we have only been dealing with rainbows when they are living in a mixed community aquarium, but if you want to you can house them in a tank specifically for rainbows. Many of my own fishes are housed this way, because my setup is primarily for breeding fish. An aquarium, however, specifically aimed at replicating an environment similar to the natural conditions these fish live under in the wild can be absolutely stunning. In Europe this sort of tank is called a biotope aquarium, and great attention is given to making sure the substrate, rocks, plants, and fishes all come from the same area. The most commonly selected regions for these biotope aquaria to be based upon are Asia and the Amazon. This is because the plants and fishes from these areas are most commonly available through the trade, so the armchair aquarist will not have to do much more than pop down to his local aquarium store to select everything he needs.

A rainbowfish biotope aquarium is more difficult to create, because rainbowfishes come from such diverse habitats. Most of the commonly kept species inhabit areas that are the homes of only a few of the plants seen in the trade. In fact, most rainbowfish keepers settle for plants that do well in the typical conditions rainbows like, e.g. moving, hard, slightly alkaline water. This gives us a wide range of species to choose from and plenty of different leaf forms and plant sizes.

***Hygrophila corymbosa* is a plant suitable for the rainbowfish aquarium.**

PHOTO BY MP&C PIEDNOIR.

***Sagittaria graminea* is suitable for the rainbowfish aquarium.**

PHOTO BY MP&C PIEDNOIR.

Towards the back and sides of the tank any of the *Sagittaria*, *Myriophyllum*, *Hygrophila*, or *Vallisneria* species can be used. Some *Cabomba* species will also grow in these sorts of conditions, but others will not. It is a case of try them and see what happens. For the foreground some *Cryptocoryne* species will adapt to the conditions, as will many *Anubias* and *Eleocharis* species. If you are really lucky you may find some Clover Fern (*Marsilea drummondii*) for sale. This is a native of Australia and soon grows to create a "lawn-like" effect at the front of an aquarium. Finally as a centerpiece you can use an Amazon Sword. There are many different species of these plants in the trade; some of them will not adapt to the conditions

Eleocharis acicularis.

PHOTO BY ANDRE ROTH.

listed, but others will. Once again it is a case of experimentation.

The trick with planting any tank is to try as many different species as possible at the start and then see which do best. Always plant them in groups of four or five plants (except large centerpiece plants like Amazon Swords) and try to find out the lighting conditions they prefer. It is useless positioning a plant that requires bright lighting in a dark corner. It will just fade away and die in a few weeks or so.

Your choice of substrates is also quite diverse. Since most of the rainbows we keep come from rivers, it is probably best to use a small to medium-size natural pea gravel. For rockwork select rounded stones rather than flat pieces of slate, and try to find a color that is contained in your gravel. Since some stones are not suitable for aquarium use it is wise to buy yours only from an aquarium shop. They might cost more than from other sources, but at least you can be sure they will be safe for your fish.

When it comes to which rainbowfishes to keep in a specialist setup you can go down one of two routes. You can have a variety of species in the tank or just have a group of one species. Obviously the more interesting setup is a mixed community of rainbows, and this will be the one most people opt for. In this sort of tank you can keep almost any of the rainbowfish species you want, because they will all live happily

Cabomba furcata.

PHOTO BY W. TOMEY.

together. The only limiting factor on this will be the size difference between the very smallest and the very largest. Some of the very large species may be tempted to make a meal of the very smallest.

For the purist, a community of rainbows in a biotope aquarium should only contain species that live together naturally, as for example a community containing *Cairnsichthys rhombosomoides, Pseudomugil signifer, Melanotaenia macculochi,* and *Melanotaenia splendida splendida.* These rainbows occur together in small rivers between Innisfail and Cairns in North Queensland and would make a very attractive community of fish with a variety of sizes, body shapes, and color forms.

The major problem with this sort of setup is that if you want to breed your rainbows you will have to remove the adults of one species to a separate breeding tank. This is because mixed communities of rainbows in captivity often hybridize. To overcome this problem many breeders house their fish in single-species tanks. These tanks are set up in the same way as a mixed community, but only one species is housed in it. This way when the fish spawn the eggs can be harvested and hatched in a separate breeding tank without any worry about what the babies will turn out to be. Some species

The rainbowfish in this tank are flourishing even though they are in a mixed community of fishes from South America, Africa and Asia.

will even flock-breed this way, with fry of different sizes growing up with their parents. Many *Pseudomugil* species will breed this way, as will some of the smaller *Melanotaenia* species.

The only problem with an aquarium containing only rainbowfishes is that they do not generally feed from the bottom, so any food that drops down will settle into the gravel and rot. Careful feeding will help prevent this problem, but it is important to make sure you regularly go over the gravel with a gravel cleaner every week or two as well.

PURCHASING AND TRANSPORTING RAINBOWS

Although most rainbows are fairly hardy and would normally transport without any problems, they can suffer chronic stress if crowded into a small bag. Personally, I always use over-sized bags and keep the numbers of fish down to the minimum. If I am transporting pairs for auction, I try to single-bag each fish and tie the two bags together. Then if anything happens to one fish the other one will still be all right and can be added to another pair or sold separately.

Looking at some of the species not yet seen in the hobby, some members of the family Atherinidae are really problematic to transport. Despite being widespread in Mexico they have very rarely been brought back alive. This is because many of these fishes die within minutes of being caught. I have managed to bring one or two species back

Amano designed, executed and photographed this tank which is ideal for rainbowfishes.

alive but only in limited numbers and never in a breedable group.

Many rainbowfish eggs, on the other hand, are tough as old boots and can safely be handled out of water, provided they don't have a chance to dry out. In many ways they are similar to killifish eggs and, in just the same way as killifish eggs, are shipped around the world by post. Many rainbowfish eggs have been flying about in recent years. That is how many of the rainbowfishes in the USA and Europe made the jump from their native shores.

To post eggs this way you will need a box made from 1-inch-thick polystyrene (Styrofoam, etc.) and some watertight vials. First of all place some strands of nylon wool, similar to those used in spawning mops, in the vials and add clean aquarium water from the breeding tank. Collect clear recently laid eggs of the desired species and place them in the vials. Next add a few more strands of wool on the top and remove enough water so that the vial is half full of water. Screw on the lids and pack them into the box so that they cannot move about. Seal the lid down and label the box ready for posting. If you are sending several orders on the same day, it is a good idea to deal with each one separately. I packed two orders at the same time on one occasion and then mixed up the labeling. Fortunately the buyers wanted mostly the same species, so it was not the disaster it could have been—but it just goes to show how easy it is to make mistakes.

FOODS AND FEEDING

In the wild, rainbows generally feed on a range of aquatic insects and their larvae, together with any terrestrial insects that fall onto the water's surface. Ants are particularly prone to falling victim to this sort of end and often make up a significant proportion of the stomach contents of wild-caught rainbows.

In captivity they will feed on just about anything the owner puts into the tank. This makes feeding them probably too easy for the fishes' long-term health. This is because the temptation is to just use a flake or granular food all the time. In some cases people feed only one brand for years on end. To a certain extent this would not matter if all foods were equally good and contained the perfect balance of nutriments for your fish. In reality some brands are lacking in one or more nutritional requirements, and long-term feeding with one of these will lead to poor growth and color, a slowdown in reproductive performance, and general weakness. In extreme cases it may even lead to premature death.

Tubifex worms are excellent IF AND ONLY IF they are fresh and clean. If there are any white-colored worms, the whole batch should be discarded.

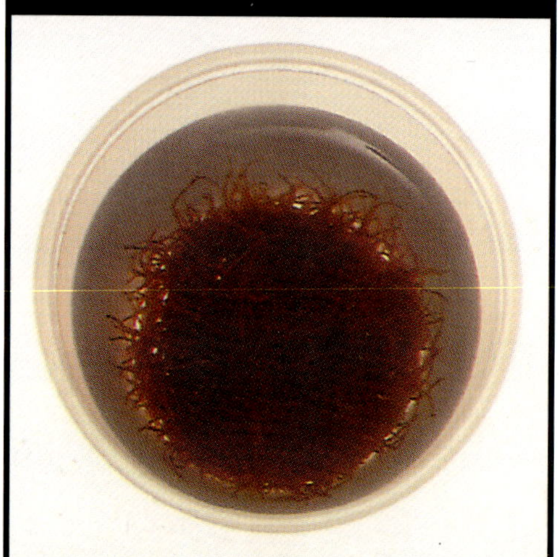

PHOTO BY ISABELLE FRANCAIS.

To prevent problems of this type, switch brands from time to time and only buy good quality commercial foods in the first place. The price is often the best guide when it comes to selecting a flake food. There are few true bargains in this world, and the makers of suspiciously cheap fish foods often cut corners to save money.

The other most important factor is to include as much live food in your fishes' diet as possible. Bloodworms, *Daphnia*, glass worms, etc., can all be purchased from your local aquarium shop or collected from local ponds. Mosquito larvae can be collected from any stagnant body of water during the summer months; a water barrel in the garden is a really good source. Alternatively, you can culture white or Grindal worms indoors. These worms have the added bonus of being free from aquatic parasites, but since they sink to the bottom fairly quickly you may have problems with pollution if you over-feed with them. Another live food particularly useful for the smaller species is newly hatched brine shrimp. Any species up to 2 inches long will eat these tiny shrimps; even larger fishes will gobble them up, but it is difficult to feed the larger fish enough to satisfy them.

During the winter months, when live foods can be hard to come by, you can use frozen alternatives. These alternatives are not as good as the live versions, but they keep your fishes in good condition. The commercially produced brands can be expensive, but if you have a good source of *Daphnia* or other live food during the summer you can freeze some of your own for nothing. I usually collect enough during the late summer months to feed most of my stock right through the winter and into spring when the ponds refill with live foods of all kinds.

Personally, I like to feed my adult fishes twice a day and any fry three or even four times a day. The first feed of the day is always a live food or frozen alternative. This is followed by a good quality commercial flake food later in the day. Fry receive newly hatched brine shrimp for their first feed, followed by two feeds of powdered fry foods or growth foods, depending on how big they are. Never crush up a general flake food to feed fry instead of feeding a specifically developed fry food. This is because the nutritional requirements of young fishes are different from those of adults. Babies reared on adult food rarely grow well and often remain stunted and have poor color.

Foods based on nutritious marine algae contain vitamin and mineral elements lacking in other foods and make good supplemental feedings for rainbowfishes and other freshwater fishes. Photo courtesy of Ocean Nutrition.

FRY FOODS

There are a number of foods that are really useful for feeding to the fry of rainbowfishes, but most of them need to be cultured or hatched rather than purchased ready-made from the local aquarium shop. The following are some of the most useful.

Green Water. The bloom of green algae that develops in ponds and standing pools of water is a really useful food for the very tiny fry of some rainbowfish species. This is easily cultured by putting some clean aquarium water in a jar and leaving it where it will receive several hours of direct sunlight per day. Out in a garden somewhere or on a bright windowsill is a good place. After a few weeks the water will turn pea green and you can use it to feed some of your youngsters on. It is

High-quality protein is an essential ingredient in fish food. Vitamin C, Spirulina and other feeding attractors add to the nutritional package, assuring that your fish will eat properly. Photo courtesy of O.S.I.Marine Lab.,Inc.

a good idea to have several jars on the go at once so you can use them in succession.

Infusoria. This is the name given to a range of single-celled organisms that feed on the bacteria produced by rotting vegetation. They are an excellent first food for many of the smaller rainbowfish fry. To start a culture of them, simply place a small piece of banana skin in a jar of aquarium water and leave it to stand for a week or two. A hazy bloom will soon develop, and it is this that you need to feed the fry by pouring some of the culture water into the tank and replacing with fresh tank water. Once again use a succession of jars and take care not to overfeed and pollute the water.

Microworms. These small worms live on the surface of cereal-based products. Porridge is the one most commonly used and also is one of the longer lasting ones. To start a culture of microworms you will have to beg or buy a starter culture, which are often offered through mail order ads. You should be able to see the tiny worms writhing on the surface of the culture medium.

First of all make up some porridge as usual and allow it to cool. Alternatively you can grind the raw porridge down in a blender until it is a powder and then just add water to it. The idea is to make a thick paste of it. A 1-inch layer of this is then placed in a plastic tub (I use old margarine tubs). A small spoonful of the old

PHOTO BY MICHAEL GILROY.

Whiteworms make excellent live foods for rainbowfishes.

Living brine shrimp is an excellent food for rainbowfishes of any age. Newly hatched shrimp are for newly hatched rainbowfish.

PHOTO BY ISABELLE FRANCAIS.

culture material is added to the mixture and the top of the container put on. (The top should have a few holes punched in it). After a few days to a week the worms will be so numerous they will start climbing up the sides of the container and congregating. From here they can be wiped off with a finger or piece of sponge and fed directly to your fry.

Brine Shrimp. Newly hatched brine shrimp are one of the best foods on the market for small fry, and with a little practice they can be very easy to hatch. First of all, though, you will need to track down a good source of eggs. Get the best available, and keep in mind that eggs from different sources are not necessarily all of the same quality. I personally avoid the eggs that have been de-shelled.

Once you have your eggs you will need a suitable hatching container and a source of air. Some companies offer special brine shrimp hatchers, but to be honest I have never bothered with them . I just use a small demijohn filled with salt water made up at the rate of five tablespoons of non-iodized salt per gallon of water. A tablespoon of eggs is then added and a rigid piece of airline put in to agitate the water. Most people use fewer eggs and a

Brine shrimp eggs are brown when dried and are sold in small vials or in bulk in larger-sized containers. They can stay alive for many years if kept dry.

PHOTO BY ISABELLE FRANCAIS.

Most, if not all, professional fish hatcheries maintain many cultures of brine shrimp. This is the brine shrimp set-up of a major private breeder.

smaller container. At a temperature of 75 F. most of the eggs will have hatched after just 24 hours, but to be sure I leave them 48 hours. Then the air is switched off and things left to settle out. The empty egg shells will float to the surface, while the shrimps and any unhatched eggs settle on the bottom. The shrimps are then siphoned out of the demijohn through a cotton handkerchief. The salt water passes through the handkerchief, leaving the shrimps ready to feed. I have two jars on the go all the time.

DISEASES

Rainbowfishes are remarkably disease-free, but they can suffer from all the usual ailments that affect freshwater tropicals. Since many of these diseases are associated with stress or poor water quality it is unlikely that your fishes will suffer from them unless the tank conditions deteriorate or they have been recently transported. For this reason proper quarantine procedures are important no matter how experienced or knowledgeable about fish you are or indeed what species are involved.

After a decade or so of fishkeeping I felt I had come across most fish diseases and could cure them without too much trouble, so I stopped bothering with quarantining new stock before introducing them to my established tanks. That proved to be one of the most disastrous mistakes I have ever made; I lost a tank full of beautiful fish through it. Since some of them were my breeding stock I lost years of work as well as the fish themselves. Nowadays I quarantine everything that comes into my setup for at least two weeks before introducing them to any established community..

Some shops claim to quarantine their fishes before they sell them. This period may be as long as two weeks or as short as one day. Either way it does not affect your need to quarantine for two weeks every fish you buy. This is because even the stress of moving them from the local shop to your home may be enough to bring out a latent disease.

One disease that seems to affect some of the captive-bred fishes in the European trade is body ulcers. The ulcers start as whitish marks underneath the skin and eventually develop into open sores on the fish's body. From my discussions with those who have had fishes that developed ulcers, it seems that they are virtually impossible to cure. The only "remedy" has been to put the fish down.

I have never seen these ulcers on fish of my own breeding, so I suspect that the organism that causes them is picked up in the over-crowded tanks of some commercial establishments. To prevent the introduction of this sort of problem to your tanks it is a good idea when buying stock to take a very close look at them. Advanced ulcers are clearly visible on the body, but the early stages also can be spotted if you look at the fish in good lighting, particularly if the light is coming from behind the fish.

Melanotaenia japenensis. This close up shot shows the teeth.

PHOTO BY DR. GERALD R. ALLEN.

A *Bedotia geayi* showing ulcer disease.

PHOTO BY RUDA ZUKAL.

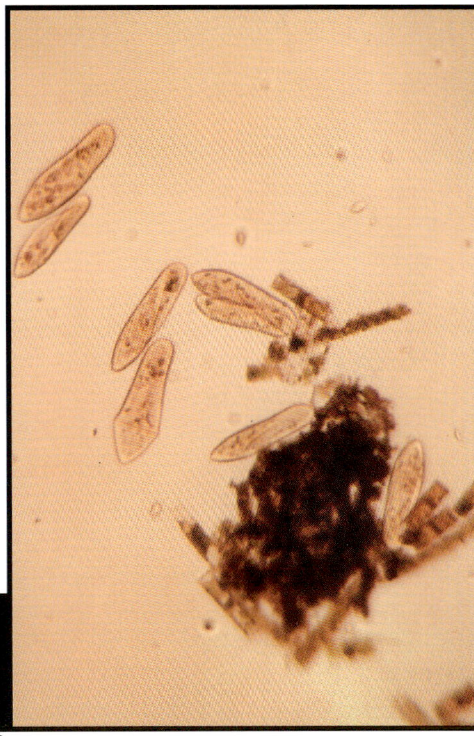

Paramecium are small organisms that make excellent food for newly hatched rainbowfishes. You need a microscope (12X) to be able to see them.

PHOTO BY MASTERS.

Ulcer disease on a *Melanotaenia*.

BREEDING RAINBOWS

SEXING RAINBOWFISHES

Most rainbowfish species are easy to sex, with males generally being the more colorful sex and very much higher-backed and/or deeper-chested. In addition, the fins are often a different shape. Males have longer and more pointed dorsal and anal fins than the females, whose fins generally are more rounded; the females also have fuller bodies. The males of some species develop long filaments on one or both dorsal fins as well as the anal fin. These filaments are often highly colored and present from a fairly young age.

In certain species, however, sexing will still be unclear until you take a close look at the first dorsal fin. In most male rainbows this fin is longer and more pointed, so much so that when it is folded back close to the body it overlaps the start of the second dorsal fin. This only happens in males and is a certain sign of sex in species such as *Melanotaenia boesemani* and *Melanotaenia trifasciata*.

Breeding rainbows is generally fairly easy, but there are differences between the various families, and there are species that have a reputation for being real problem fish. Fishes from some of the families in the order Atheriniformes, however, have never been bred in captivity, and very little is known about their reproductive strategies.

Melanotaenia boesemani spawner near the artificial mop in which eggs are visible.

PHOTO BY HANS JOACHIM RICHTER.

A male *Melanotaenia* with fins extended. A female would have more rounded anal and dorsal fins.

PHOTO BY W.SOMMER.

In general if you want to breed most rainbowfishes you will need at least one separate tank in which to hatch and rear the babies. This should be about 24 inches long and contain a small aerating sponge filter. If the species concerned is a large one (four inches and over), I use a 36-inch aquarium instead. I don't use any substrate in my breeding tanks, which generally will be freshly set up for each breeding attempt after having been thoroughly cleaned out with very hot (at least by aquarium maintenance standards) water beforehand. You of course have to be careful in applying hot water to glass surfaces generally, and you have to be especially careful if the glass is cold.

I try to position my breeding tanks where they will receive as much morning sunlight as possible, because this encourages rainbows to spawn. With only one small window in my fish room, it's difficult to position more than a tank or two in morning sunlight, and most of them have to make do with basic fluorescent lights.

I tend to use nylon wool mops as a spawning medium, but other breeders prefer to use natural plants like Java Moss or Cabomba. My reason for not using these plants myself is because they can not be properly sterilized before being put into the aquarium. Nylon wool mops can be soaked in very hot salty water for about one hour, which will kill most bacteria and parasites. The mops are then rinsed under running cold water and wrung out before being placed into the breeding tank. Depending upon the species concerned, the mops will either be hung from one end of the tank to create the effect of plant roots hanging down in the water or scattered over the tank bottom like low-growing plants.

Apart from the spawning mops and an aerating sponge filter, the tank is usually left bare. In the evening a well conditioned pair of rainbows will be placed in the breeding tank. Most will spawn the next morning at first light, but some may take a few days to start breeding after the move. Most rainbows spawn just about every day, but some will breed once every few weeks. Either way I leave the pair set up for about a week before removing them or the mops. Each family and even individual species within a family breed in a slightly different way, so it is important to try experimenting with different techniques to see which is the most successful.

The family of rainbows whose members are most often bred in captivity is Melanotaeniidae, which includes most of the commonly found Australian and New Guinea rainbowfishes. They are generally very productive, with one spawning numbering as many as 200 or more eggs. The eggs tend to be small and are deposited amongst fine-leafed plants or floating plant roots shortly after daybreak. For these species I tend to use spawning mops hung from one end of the aquarium. Most pairs

Glossolepis incisus male flirting with a female.

PHOTO BY HANS JOACHIM RICHTER.

The male *Glossolepis incisus* leads the female into the bushes where they will deposit their eggs.

PHOTO BY HANS JOACHIM RICHTER.

A pair of *Glossolepis* embracing as they release sperm and eggs.

PHOTO BY HANS JOACHIM RICHTER.

The eggs are well scattered after spawning of *Glossolepis incisus.*

PHOTO BY HANS JOACHIM RICHTER.

Freshly laid eggs of *Glossolepis incisus*.

PHOTO BY MP&C PIEDNOIR.

The egg of *Glossolepis incisus* immediately prior to hatching.

PHOTO BY MP&C PIEDNOIR.

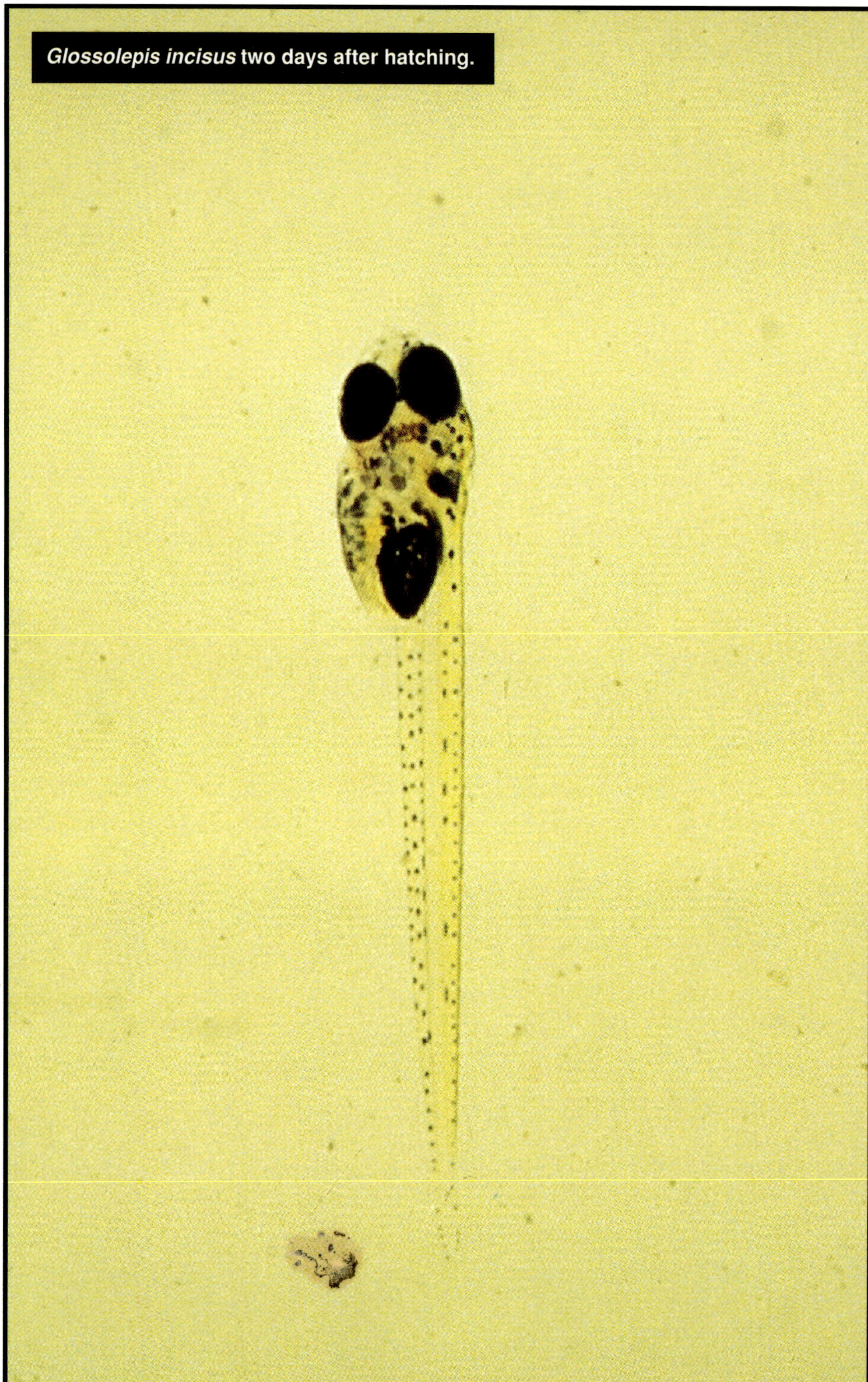

Glossolepis incisus two days after hatching.

PHOTO BY MP&C PIEDNOIR.

spawn into the mops, with the pair swimming up from the bottom of the mop towards the top, releasing eggs and milt into the mop as they go. When they reach the surface they normally slip sideways away from each other and swim away. Some pairs, however, have a habit of jumping right out of the water in their excitement. For this reason it is very important to keep the breeding tank covered tightly above this area.

The eggs take about a week to hatch, and the fry of most species are so small they need very tiny foods if they are to survive. Very fine powdered fry food will be taken by the larger fry, but in general they need liquid fry foods or infusoria for the first week or two. This should be fed carefully so as not to pollute the water and kill the delicate babies.

As soon as the fry look large enough to take newly hatched brine shrimp, this should be added to their diet. To start with feed just a little of this excellent food and look at the fry closely. If they are eating it they will develop full stomachs with an orange flush to them. Once you are sure all the babies are large enough to manage the shrimps, the liquid food can be discontinued and powdered fry food included in the diet. Brine shrimp should constitute the bulk of their diet at this stage. Later, larger commercial growth foods can replace the powdered food. It is important to feed only growth or fry foods designed specifically for those purposes and not just grind down the flakes designed for adults. The reason for this is that the growth foods should have different nutritional values to take account of young fishes' accelerated growth rates. Using adult foods for fry will lead to the youngsters' growing slowly and remaining smaller than they should, often with poorer color.

The next most commonly bred family of rainbows is Pseudomugilidae. The males of many pseudomugilid species stake out their own territory centered on a suitable spawning site. In this case I use a single mop hung from each end of the aquarium and another mop placed directly under each of these. Into this setup I place two males and a group of six females if I have them available. The males will take up positions at either end of the tank, with the dominant male usually having the mop closest to the window.

Every morning, after the breeding group has been fed, ripe females will be attracted to the mops by the courting males. They then lay 1 to 12 eggs into the mop. Most species will use the suspended mop to deposit their eggs in, but some prefer the mop lying under the upper mop.

Despite their diminutive size, the eggs produced by most of these fishes are quite large (1mm+) and can be carefully picked off the mops every day or two. I place them into another tank for hatching and rearing. This way I can have a succession of babies growing up in the

A male *Pseudomugil signifer* with extended fins.

PHOTO BY HANS JOACHIM RICHTER.

A pair of *Pseudomugil signifer*.

PHOTO BY HANS JOACHIM RICHTER.

A pair of *Pseudomugil signifer* chasing into the bushes.

PHOTO BY HANS JOACHIM RICHTER.

A group spawning of *Pseudomugil signifer*.

PHOTO BY HANS JOACHIM RICHTER.

rearing tank and a permanent breeding group. It is worth remembering that none of these fish are particularly long-lived, and you should aim to replace the breeding group every four to six months with younger fish. Their prime breeding age seems to be between six and ten months of age.

Two other families of rainbows are regularly bred in captivity, but both of these families are represented by only one species each at the moment. In Atherinidae we have only the Madagascan rainbowfish, *Bedotia geayi*, currently. This species can be bred in much the same manner as those of Melanotaeniidae. The mops should be suspended from the surface and the pair left in the breeding setup for up to ten days before removing them.

The fry tend to swim with their heads angled upwards when they first hatch, which can be a little disconcerting when you first see it. Within a few days they will have attained a normal swimming position and will be feeding on infusoria. They are very sensitive to poor water quality, so you have to balance feeding enough food for the babies to eat properly while at the same time not feeding too much and polluting the water.

The final species regularly bred in captivity is *Telmatherina ladigesi*, one of the Sulawesi rainbows of the family Telmatherinidae. The females produce quite large eggs, which are laid into suspended mops first

Chilatherina fasciata.

PHOTOS BY HANS JOACHIM RICHTER.

This series of photos shows *Chilatherina fasciata* before, during and after spawning while the male first gains, then loses color and the female shows varying degrees of cooperation.

PHOTOS BY HANS JOACHIM RICHTER.

thing in the morning. Since this species tends to be an egg-eater, it is best to search through the mops at lunch time or during the early afternoon and pick out any eggs you find. They can be hatched and reared in a separate tank, with the adults housed in the permanent breeding setup. The fry are usually quite large and may be able to take brine shrimp right from the start, but they may need infusoria for the fist week. Which first food the fry will be able to take depends mostly on how big the adult female is. Larger females tend to produce more but smaller eggs.

Some of the other families of rainbows have fascinating reproductive strategies that aquarists have yet to really have the opportunity to observe. The members of the family Phallostethidae have probably the most unusual reproductive strategies. In these fishes part of the body has developed into a copulatory organ called a priapium. The priapium is positioned just behind the head rather than near the anal fin, where you would normally expect to find such an organ. There is sometimes also a slender anterior projection and one or two posterior projections that are possibly used to hold onto the female during mating. The females also have some unique adaptations, including a scale over the urogenital opening, which also is positioned below the throat. Very strange fish indeed; they have yet to make their mark on the hobby.

Telmatherina ladigesi.

PHOTO BY HANS JOACHIM RICHTER

A series of spawning sequences showing the breeding behavior of *Telmatherina ladigesi*. This photo shows a pair preparing to spawn.

PHOTOS IN THIS SERIES BY HANS JOACHIM RICHTER.

The egg-laden female being lead into the thickets.

After eggs have been expelled, the male and female separate.

The spawning partners continue to drift apart.

When spawning is over, the female retreats from the male.
PHOTO BY HANS JOACHIM RICHTER.

THE IMPORTANCE OF GEOGRAPHIC VARIETIES AND SPECIALIST SOCIETIES.

Many species of rainbows with a wide geographic distribution have different color forms in each river. With the rapid pace of scientific research, some of these color forms will eventually be given status as separate species, so if you breed two different geographic varieties together you will, in effect, be creating hybrids. These hybrids have no scientific value; being only a half-way house between two species, they have little to recommend them to the serious hobbyist. It is therefore important to keep members of each species and each geographic location separate for breeding purposes. That way, if anything happens to the natural habitat of the fish concerned, the original form can be re-introduced once the problem existing in the natural habitat has been solved. Re-introduction may already be necessary with one species of rainbow and may be needed with many more in the future as a result of environmental damage and the introduction of exotic species.

What this means to the serious rainbowfish breeder is that many of the fishes sold through normal aquatic outlets are useless for breeding purposes. These fishes rarely have the collection point given with them, and if they do they are not necessarily correct. In some cases, in fact, incorrect locations might be provided deliberately.

If you really want to breed rainbowfishes seriously, it will be important for you to join a specialist society. In the United Kingdom we have the British Rainbow And Goby Society, while in America there is The Rainbowfish Study Group, Inc. Other groups around the world include the Internationale Gesellschaft Fur Regenbogenfische, which is an international organization widespread in Europe and run from Germany, and the Australia New Guinea Fishes Association (ANGFA) which is the oldest and best-established of all these specialist societies. ANGFA is centered in Australia and seems to produce the best material of all of them. Current addresses can be found in the aquatic press.

THE AQUARIST'S ROLE IN CONSERVATION

The Lake Eacham Rainbowfish, *Melanotaenia eachamensis*, more than any other rainbowfish, shows the importance of the aquarist in regard to captive breeding and conservation. In 1987 it was discovered that this rainbowfish had died out in its only known range due to the introduction of four species of fishes from outside Lake Eacham. Thanks to several Australian aquarists who had maintained the fish in captivity, stock could be obtained by the professional conservation organizations and public zoos with which to launch a re-introduction program. The first trial was undertaken with 1000 fish a few years ago but seems to have failed.

Melanotaenia eachemensis.

The probable reason for this failure was that no attempt had been made to remove the introduced species first. Just how you would undertake such a project without seriously damaging the rest of the wildlife that inhabits this area is difficult to say, but it must be done before *M. eachamensis* can be re-established in its native habitat.

Fortunately more extensive studies of the fish that live in this general area have recently proved that there are two other populations of this species alive and well in the wild, so this story has a happy ending for now—but it does show just how important captive breeding by aquarists is today and will be in the future.

COMMON SPECIES IN THE HOBBY

Of the 277 species and 7 families of rainbowfishes, only some 20 species in 4 families are commonly seen in the hobby outside of specialist society auctions; there are even fewer rainbowfish species normally sold in aquarium shops. Despite this limited number of species, almost the full diversity of the group is available to those who search them out. The following are some of the more popular species at the moment:-

ATHERINIDAE

Bedotia geayi, Madagascan Rainbowfish

This is one of the larger rainbows; it can reach 6 inches in body length. It fits in well with most peaceful fishes of a similar size and can adapt to soft water. It needs plenty of live food in its diet and is intolerant of poor water conditions, so it is recommended for the more experienced hobbyist.

Bedotia geayi, a pair, with the male the lower of the two fish.

PHOTO BY HANS JOACHIM RICHTER.

Glossolepis incisus, male.

PHOTO BY HANS JOACHIM RICHTER.

MELANOTAENIIDAE

Glossolepis incisus, Red Rainbowfish

This is one of the largest of the rainbows, reaching a maximum size of 6 inches in captivity. Males are almost totally red, while females are silvery. Needs alkaline conditions to do well, and males can be aggressive towards females and weaker males. Eats all foods and is one of the species most commonly seen in aquarium shops.

Iriatherina werneri, Threadfin Rainbowfish

When this diminutive species (maximum size 2 inches) first hit the hobby it was an instant hit. While hardy once established in an aquarium, it must be carefully and slowly acclimated to different water conditions whenever transferred. Eats all small foods and can be combined with other small peaceful species. Best suited to the more advanced hobbyist.

Two male *Iriatherina werneri* displaying before female.

PHOTO BY MP&C PIEDNOIR.

Iriatherina werneri, a male.

PHOTO BY MP&C PIEDNOIR.

Melanotaenia fluviatilis female.

PHOTO BY ANDRE ROTH.

Melanotaenia fluviatilis, Murray River Rainbowfish

This fish was first introduced to the UK hobby in the mid-1960s and was commonly available for a few years. After that it disappeared until recently. It grows to just over 3 inches in captivity, although it may reach 4 inches in the wild. This is one of the few rainbows adapted to low winter temperatures. Water temperatures below 50 F are known in the areas where this fish is found.

Melanotaenia boesemani.

PHOTO BY MP&C PIEDNOIR.

Melanotaenia boesemani, Boeseman's Rainbowfish

Reaching about 4.5 inches in length in captivity, this lovely bicolored fish has become one of the most popular species of the genus. It accepts most water conditions from slightly acidic through to very alkaline and will do well when combined with peaceful fishes of a similar size. It can be recommended for the beginner.

Melanotaenia herbertaxelrodi from Lake Tebera during spawning.

PHOTO BY NEIL ARMSTRONG.

Melanotaenia herbertaxelrodi, Lake Tebera Rainbowfish

This species is one of the most colorful members of the genus from New Guinea. It reaches a maximum size of 5 inches in captivity and eats all foods. It prefers slightly alkaline water and a cooler temperature range between 70 and 76 degrees F.

Melanotaenia lacustris.

PHOTO BY MP&C PIEDNOIR.

Melanotaenia maccullochi.

Melanotaenia nigrans.

PHOTO BY DR. GERALD R. ALLEN.

Melanotaenia praecox.

PHOTO BY DR. GERALD R. ALLEN.

Melanotaenia lacustris, Lake Kutubu Rainbowfish

If you like blue fishes, you really must have this species. The entire upper half of the body is an intense turquoise blue, fading into white on the stomach. Fully grown at about 5 inches, *M. lacustris* is suitable for a community tank and is recommended for the beginner.

Melanotaenia maccullochi, MacCulloch's Rainbowfish or Dwarf Australian Rainbowfish

One of the very earliest introductions to the aquarium hobby. This is a hardy peaceful species that grows to about 3 inches when fully grown. Eats all foods and can be housed in most community tanks. It is recommended for the beginner.

Melanotaenia nigrans, Black-banded Rainbowfish

This is one of the smaller species of rainbow; it reaches only 3 inches in captivity. For many years *Melanotaenia duboulayi* was sold as this species throughout Europe and even now many books show the wrong fish accompanying discussions of this species. It is peaceful and eats all foods. An ideal inmate for a mixed community tank.

Melanotaenia praecox, Dwarf Neon Rainbowfish

This is one of the smallest in the genus, reaching only 2.25 inches in length when fully grown. It was a smash hit when first introduced to the aquarium hobby and has maintained its popularity ever since. Eats all foods and is a prolific breeder that can be flock-bred in a well planted aquarium. Well suited to a community aquarium and is recommended for the beginner.

Melanotaenia splendida australis, Western Rainbowfish

This fish has recently become a common fish in the trade. It is one of the most abundant of all rainbows and is hardy and easy to keep in captivity. Grows to about 4 inches in body length and is ideal for beginners.

Melanotaenia splendida splendida, Eastern Rainbowfish

This is a fairly large rainbow and can reach over 5 inches in captivity. It is a highly variable species in the wild, with almost every river in its range having its own unique color form. Although easy to keep in captivity, it needs a large aquarium and does best if kept in a group of 10 to 20 fish.

Melanotaenia trifasciata, Banded Rainbowfish

This very attractive species can grow to over 5 inches in captivity. There are lots of geographic varieties having different colors, which can make positive identification a little difficult, particularly if the fish have been obtained from a trade source. Needs a large aquarium if it is to achieve its maximum potential.

PSEUDOMUGILIDAE

Pseudomugil connieae, Popondetta Rainbowfish

Less than 2 inches when fully grown, this small rainbow is a truly beautiful fish that fits in well with other small fishes in a mixed

Melanotaenia splendida australis.

PHOTO BY HANS JOACHIM RICHTER.

Melanotaenia splendida splendida.

Melanotaenia trifasciata.

Pseudomugil connieae. Named by Dr. Allen to honor his wife.

PHOTO BY HANS JOACHIM RICHTER.

Pseudomugil signifer with fins erect.

PHOTO BY HANS JOACHIM RICHTER.

Pseudomugil signifer.

PHOTO BY HANS JOACHIM RICHTER.

community. Providing they are transferred over slowly they will adapt to a wide range of water conditions ranging from soft and slightly acidic to hard and alkaline.

Pseudomugil furcatus, Forked-Tail Rainbowfish

This species is very similar to *Pseudomugil connieae* but has yellow in the fins rather than white, and the top and bottom lobes of the caudal fin are edged in black. Aquarium care is similar for both species.

Pseudomugil gertrudae, Spotted Blue-eye

This is one of the smallest of all rainbows, reaching a maximum size of only 1.5 inches in captivity. It will tolerate very acidic to moderately alkaline conditions.

Pseudomugil signifer, Pacific Blue-eye

This species reaches about 2.5 inches in captivity and is a very active fish that does well in a community tank. It prefers slightly alkaline water but can tolerate a wide temperature range, from 68 - 80F.

TELMATHERINIDAE

Telmatherina ladigesi, Celebes Rainbowfish

The Celebes rainbowfish has been a popular aquarium fish ever since it was first introduced to the hobby in 1933. It grows to only about 3 inches and will live happily with most fishes of a similar size and temperament. It prefers slightly alkaline hard water and plenty of plant growth.

Pseudomugil gertrudae.

PHOTO BY HANS JOACHIM RICHTER.

Telmatherina ladigesi.

PHOTO BY ANDRE ROTH

INDEX

Page numbers in **boldface** refer to illustrations.